Ladybird

Acknowledgments

page 7, Jane Taylor, *Twinkle, Twinkle, Little Star;*
page 17, Alfred, Lord Tennyson, *Sweet and Low;*
page 19, Johannes Brahms, *Cradle Song*.

Material in this book was previously published in Ladybird's *Nursery Rhymes* gift book.

Ladybird books are widely available, but in case of
difficulty may be ordered by post or telephone from:

Ladybird Books – Cash Sales Department
Littlegate Road Paignton Devon TQ3 3BE
Telephone 01803 554761

A catalogue record for this book is available
from the British Library

Published by Ladybird Books Ltd Loughborough Leicestershire UK
Ladybird Books Inc Auburn Maine 04210 USA

BEDTIME
RHYMES

Chosen by Ronne Randall
Illustrated by Peter Stevenson

The evening is coming,
The sun sinks to rest,
The birds are all flying
Straight home to the nest.
"Caw," says the crow
As he flies overhead,
"It's time little children
Were going to bed!"

Now the day is over,
Night is drawing nigh.
Shadows of the evening
Steal across the sky.

Down with the lambs,
Up with the lark,
Run to bed, children,
Before it gets dark.

Quiet the night,
Soft is the breeze.
Dim is the light
Of the faraway moon.

Sleep, children, sleep,
Be not alarmed,
Angels on guard
Will keep you unharmed.

Twinkle, twinkle, little star,
How I wonder what you are!
Up above the world so high,
Like a diamond in the sky.

When the blazing sun is gone,
When he nothing shines upon,
Then you show your little light,
Twinkle, twinkle, all the night.

Star light,
Star bright,
First star I see tonight,
I wish I may,
I wish I might,
Have the wish
I wish tonight.

I see the moon,
And the moon sees me.
God bless the moon,
And God bless me.

The man in the moon
Looked out of the moon,
And this is what he said:
"Now that I'm getting up, 'tis time
All children went to bed!"

Wee Willie Winkie
Runs through the town,
Upstairs and downstairs
In his nightgown,
Rapping at the window,
Crying through the lock,
"Are the children all in bed,
For now it's eight o'clock!"

The Sandman comes,
The Sandman comes.
He has such pretty snow-white sand,
And well he's known throughout the land.
The Sandman comes.

Hush-a-bye, don't you cry,
Go to sleep little baby.
When you wake, you shall have
All the pretty little horses.
Blacks and bays, dapples and greys,
Coach and six little horses.

The man in the moon
Came tumbling down,
And asked the way to Norwich.

He went by south,
And burnt his mouth
With supping cold
   pease porridge.

How many miles
  to Babyland?
Anyone can tell.
Up one flight,
To your right,
Please to ring the bell.

Rock a-bye, baby,
Thy cradle is green,
Father's a nobleman,
Mother's a queen.
Betty's a lady and wears a gold ring,
And Johnny's a drummer, and
  drums for the King.

Hush, little baby,
Don't say a word,

Papa's going to buy you
a mockingbird.

If that mockingbird
won't sing,

Papa's going to buy you
a diamond ring.

If that diamond ring
turns brass,

Papa's going to buy you
a looking glass.

If that looking glass
gets broke,

Papa's going to buy you
a billy goat.

If that billy goat won't pull,

Papa's going to buy you
a cart and bull.

If that cart and bull
turn over,

Papa's going to buy you
a dog named Rover.

If that dog named Rover
won't bark,

Papa's going to buy you
a horse and cart.

If that horse and cart
fall down,

You'll still be the sweetest
little baby in town.

Bossy-cow, bossy-cow, where do you lie?
In the green meadows, under the sky.

Billy-horse, billy-horse, where do you lie?
Out in the stable, with nobody nigh.

Birdies bright, birdies sweet, where do you lie?
Up in the treetops, ever so high.

Baby dear, baby love, where do you lie?
In my warm cradle, with Mama close by.

Hush-a-bye, baby, on the treetop,
When the wind blows, the cradle will rock.
When the bough breaks, the cradle will fall,
And down will come baby, cradle and all.

Sleep, baby, sleep,
Thy father guards the sheep,
Thy mother shakes the dreamland tree,
And from it fall sweet dreams for thee.
Sleep, baby, sleep.

Sleep, baby, sleep,
Down where the woodbines creep.
Be always like the lamb so mild,
A kind and sweet and gentle child.
Sleep, baby, sleep.

Come to the window, my baby, with me,
And look at the stars that shine on the sea.
There are two little stars that play at bo-peep
With two little fishes far down in the deep,
And two little frogs cry, "Neap, neap, neap,
I see a dear baby that should be asleep!"

Sweet and low, sweet and low,
    Wind of the western sea.
Low, low, breathe and blow,
    Wind of the western sea!
Over the rolling waters go,
Come from the dying moon, and blow,
    Blow him again to me;
While my little one, while my
    pretty one, sleeps.

Rock-a-bye, baby, rock, rock, rock,
Listen, who comes with a knock, knock, knock?
Oh, it is pussy! Come in, come in!
Mother and baby are always at home.

To my baby's cradle in the night
Comes a little goat all
  snowy-white.
The goat will trot to the market,
While Mother her watch
  does keep,
Bringing back raisins and almonds.
Sleep, my little one, sleep.

Lullaby and good night, thy mother's delight,
Bright angels around my darling shall stand.
They will guard thee from harms,
Thou shalt wake in my arms.
They will guard thee from harms,
Thou shalt wake in my arms.

There was an old woman who lived in a shoe,
She had so many children she didn't know
  what to do.
She gave them some broth without any bread,
Then scolded them soundly and sent them
  to bed.

Go to bed first, a golden purse;
Go to bed second, a golden pheasant;
Go to bed third, a golden bird.

Go to bed late,
Stay very small.
Go to bed early,
Grow very tall.

Hush-a-bye, baby, lie still in the cradle,
Mother has gone to buy a soup ladle.
When she comes back, she'll bring us some meat,
And Father and baby shall have some to eat.

Hush-a-bye, baby, lie still with thy daddy,
Thy mammy has gone to the mill,
To get some meal, to make a cake,
So pray, my dear baby, lie still.

Sleep, oh sleep,
While breezes so softly
    are blowing.
Sleep, oh sleep,
While streamlets so gently
    are flowing.
Sleep, oh sleep!

Sleep, oh sleep,
While birds in the forest
    are singing.
Sleep, oh sleep,
While echoes with music
    are ringing.
Sleep, oh sleep!

Up the wooden hill
To Bedfordshire,
Down Sheet Lane
To Blanket Fair.

Diddle, diddle, dumpling, my son John
Went to bed with his trousers on.
One shoe off, and one shoe on,
Diddle, diddle, dumpling, my son John.

Teddy bear, teddy bear,
Turn around.
Teddy bear, teddy bear,
Touch the ground.
Teddy bear, teddy bear,
Climb the stairs.
Teddy bear, teddy bear,
Say your prayers.
Teddy bear, teddy bear,
Turn out the light.
Teddy bear, teddy bear,
Say good night.

If my boy sleep quietly,
He shall see the busy bee,
When it has made its honey fine,
Dancing in the bright sunshine.

If my boy will slumber,
Angels without number
Will draw near, so fair and bright,
For they only come at night.

Good night,
Sleep tight,
Wake up bright
In the morning light
To do what's right
With all your might.